The Perfect Legacy

How to Establish Your Own Private Foundation

by Russ Alan Prince

Gary L. Rathbun

Karen Maru File

The Perfect Legacy — How to Establish Your Own Private Foundation

Russ Alan Prince
Gary L. Rathbun
Karen Maru File

HNW Press

Copyright ©1998 by Russ Alan Prince and Karen Maru File

All rights reserved. No part of this book may be reproduced or transmitted in any form or by any means, electronic or mechanical, including photocopying, recording, or by any information storage and retrieval system, without permission in writing from the Publisher.

The information contained herein is accurate to the best of the publisher's knowledge; however, the publisher and authors cannot accept responsibility for the accuracy or completeness of such information or for the loss or damage caused by any use thereof. If legal, financial or other expert assistance is required, the services of a competent professional should be sought.

Except for public figures, all names and identifying information of people referenced or quoted in this book have been altered to protect their confidentiality.

HNW Press   76 Penfield Road • Fairfield, CT 06430
              Tel. 203-255-8772 • Fax 203-256-9147

Printed in the United States of America. Printing number 1

ISBN number 0-9658391-1-7

Book design by: LUNA Corporate Design
Tel. 203-378-2543 • Email: LunaCorp@aol.com

Cover illustration ©Dianne S. P. Cermak • Tel. 781-455-6334

Case writer: Lisa Novick • Email: LNovick@usc.edu

For Angel and Oliver
- Russ Alan Prince

To my good friend and counselor, Chris E. Steiner, JD
- Gary L. Rathbun

To Joe, Charlie and Mike
- Karen Maru File

About the Authors

Russ Alan Prince is President of Prince & Associates, a research and consulting firm with expertise in charitable planning and giving. Mr. Prince has consulted on charitable planning for individuals for many years, and on development issues with such organizations as the American Medical Association and the American Heart Association. He is regularly featured in the Chronicle of Philanthropy and the journal Trusts & Estates. He is co-author (with Gary Rathbun) of The Charitable Giving Handbook and co-author (with Karen File) of The Seven Faces of Philanthropy.

Gary L. Rathbun is a professional financial and charitable planner. Over his many years of professional practice, he has helped hundreds of affluent individuals with their personal estate and charitable planning over the years. He is President of Private Wealth Consultants. His particular area of expertise is private foundations, and he is co-author (with Russ Prince) of The Charitable Giving Handbook. Mr. Rathbun is frequently called upon to lead seminars on the topic.

Karen Maru File is Associate Professor of Marketing at the University of Connecticut, where a major area of her research has been philanthropy. She has been the principal investigator on several national studies of charitable giving, and has published on values and motivations associated with charitable giving in such journals as the Journal of Business Research, and Non-Profit Management and Leadership. She is co-author (with Russ Prince) of The Seven Faces of Philanthropy.

For additional information about the material in this book, please call Gary Rathbun at 1-419-473-9742.

Table of Contents

VI

Preface

We have been in the business of helping people think through charitable planning issues for years, and have been struck by how little is written from the donor's point of view. We have been asked so often for a donor handbook on foundations that covers all the material in our workshops, that we finally decided to sit down and write one.

We hope you find this book useful.

As you read the pages ahead, it is essential to keep your "big picture" in mind: the idea of your foundation, how your foundation will be in the world, how it will help others, how your family will be involved. Of course, there are countless technical details and rules, and policies and procedures, but that is why you have expert advisors. Understand the principles, as they are laid out here, and you will be able to manage your foundation well.

Russ Alan Prince
Gary L. Rathbun
Karen Maru File
April 1998

VIII

Foundations and You

*"Deserving charities exist everywhere, but it is
manifest that you cannot help all."*
- Conrad Hilton

A foundation will probably not let you save the world, but it will enable you to make a difference. People who care deeply about the world they live in, and the world they leave for their children and the future, have been turning to private foundations as an excellent way to make the difference they envision.

This book will bring you through the process of setting up a foundation. It will not be very technical, however, because we want you to focus on the important decisions. Of course, if you decide to go ahead with a foundation, you will work with professional advisors who will help you with the technical aspects.

Before we explore foundations - what they are and what they are not - let's talk about charitable giving in general, and about your personal motivations.

Why People Give

We have found that people like to see what other people do when it comes to giving. Such comparisons help stimulate new ideas or clarify existing ones.

Although the people making charitable gifts are as varied as their reasons for making them, we find that they cluster into seven groups. We have called these the *Seven Faces of Philanthropy*[1].

What are the Seven Faces of Philanthropy? They are seven types of givers. Look at the following chart and select the type that fits you most closely. Of course, there is no right or wrong type. Whatever your type of giving, all charitable giving is certainly the right thing to do.

What's Your Type?

Communitarian — Communitarians are rooted in their community and are very local and community minded. They want to make their communities stronger and more positive places.

Devout — The Devout are religiously oriented and give to causes related to their religious beliefs and practices. They want to be a part of God's work on earth.

Investor — Investors bring a business eye to their charitable giving and prefer to support charities that are well run and efficient. They look for personal tax and financial advantages for themselves as well.

Socialite — Socialites know you can do good and have a good time while doing it. Socialites like to be associated with charity fundraisers and social events.

Altruist — Altruists generally wish to remain anonymous, and avoid any public recognition of their good works. Their giving comes from their sense of self.

Repayer — Repayers give out of a sense of obligation for what they have received in life. Often, Repayers are generous donors to schools and hospitals.

Dynast — Dynasts feel that family tradition is important to giving, and that giving has always been central to their family identity.

We find that a vast majority of generous people are able to place themselves in this framework.

"I am clearly a Repayer. I've been giving to the American Cancer Society since Mother died and to the hospital that did so much for her." - PJS

"I guess I'm a Communitarian. I feel if you make your money in a community, you should put something back into the community. That's why we support Boys' and Girls' Clubs and after-school programs." - JWB

Founders of major foundations are also representatives of these types.

Charles Stewart Mott is an excellent example of a Communitarian philanthropist. He made his fortune when he moved his failing wheel factory to Flint, Michigan, just as the automobile industry was taking off. Ever grateful to his adoptive home town, he gave to many local causes before starting his foundation. From the first, the foundation concentrated on charities and causes in and around Flint, Michigan. One of the programs in which Mott took greatest pleasure was his community school program, whereby schools would be used for a wide variety of youth and adult programs. At one point, 90,000 people out of a city population of 200,000 were involved.

The Seven Faces of Philanthropy

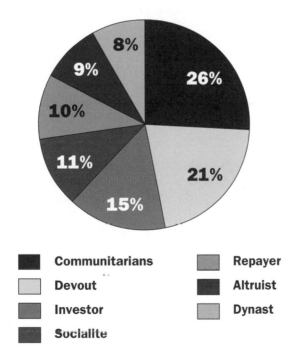

Source: Prince and File, The Seven Faces of Philanthropy

Alfred Sloan is an interesting example of a Repayer. Head of General Motors during the years of its early enormous growth, he relished business and economics for what it had done for him and for others. As a result, he founded the Sloan Foundation to further research and public understanding of economics. Later on, he joined Charles Kettering in creating the Sloan-Kettering Center for Cancer Research in New York City.

John Andrus is an example of an Altruist. A man from a disadvantaged background who became a self-made man, he started the Surdna (Andrus spelled backward) Foundation after his wife died. The original purpose of the foundation was to take care of orphans and the destitute elderly. The Foundation continues those two missions, and now also gives to education and medical causes.

Herman Brown and his wife are examples of Socialites. He made his fortune in construction in Texas, and she became an influential patron of art and music. Both he and his wife left the bulk of their estates to the Brown Foundation, which continues to be a major supporter of the Museum of Fine Arts in Houston.

People find they can be combinations of types, such as a Devout and a Dynast. They also find that they can be a different type at different points in their lives, depending on circumstances.

More people are Communitarians than any other type (26%), followed closely by the Devout (21%). Fewer people are Altruists (9%) or Dynasts (8%).

Since each type gives to charities for different reasons, it should not be surprising that they are interested in different modes of giving. Some types are interested in charitable remainder trusts, others in community foundations. However, private foundations are the one mode of giving in which they are all interested.

Should I Have a Private Foundation?

There is increasing interest in private foundations these days. A lot of people are giving serious consideration to the advantages and appeal of creating a private foundation. In the previous section, we saw that people who are already very involved in charitable giving are very interested in foundations. New research confirms this finding. We found that eight out of ten (85%) very affluent individuals (regardless of their charitable giving) are quite curious about private foundations and want to learn more about whether they would meet their needs. Only 15% are not interested.

Affluent People's Interest in Learning More About Private Foundations

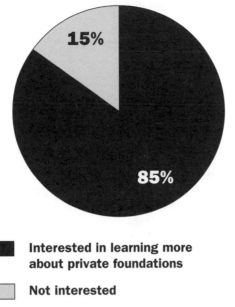

15%

85%

■ **Interested in learning more about private foundations**

☐ **Not interested**

Source: Prince, McBride and File, The Charitable Estate Planning Process

This current interest continues an important tradition in American giving. Foundations are important in American philanthropy. Not many people realize that ninety-five out of every hundred dollars that goes to a nonprofit comes from an individual. Most of that is current contributions directly from people. But an increasing portion of that giving comes from people through their foundations (see the chart below), and an additional portion comes from people through their wills.

Foundations are also important because they are concentrated sources of giving. Nine foundations give $100 million or more each and every year (as shown in the table below).

The reasons for creating a private foundation are as diverse and interesting as the individuals who create them. Just about everyone says they want to leave something worthwhile after themselves, some sort of meaningful legacy for the future.

"It sounds kind of sentimental, but I think a lot about the world Adam is growing up into, and I want to make it as safe

and happy for him and other children as I possibly can. That's why I give to the causes I do." - KDP

Giving Type	Giving Mode	% Interested
Communitarians	Life insurance	8
	Charitable remainder trust	45
	Community foundation	22
	Private foundation	100
Devout	Life insurance	5
	Charitable remainder trust	48
	Community foundation	0
	Private foundation	100
Investors	Life insurance	14
	Charitable remainder trust	36
	Community foundation	15
	Private foundation	100
Socialites	Life insurance	7
	Charitable remainder trust	53
	Community foundation	0
	Private foundation	100
Repayers	Life insurance	9
	Charitable remainder trust	49
	Community foundation	0
	Private foundation	100
Altruists	Life insurance	7
	Charitable remainder trust	20
	Community foundation	0
	Private foundation	100
Dynasts	Life insurance	0
	Charitable remainder trust	42
	Community foundation	0
	Private foundation	100

Source: Prince and File, The Seven Faces of Philanthropy

"I want to be remembered as someone who cared a lot about beauty. For me, art is very precious, and artists are very important. I wanted to do something to help art and artists in the future."- SMH

The types of legacies people want to leave are about as diverse as the people themselves. Some, like Bob and Julie, want to help make a better world in some way by taking on social problems. Others, like Suzanne and Fred, want a more beautiful and inspiring world, and so they help artists. Others, like Linda, want a hopeful and safe world, and so they focus on children. Still other philanthropists, like Ivan and Jean, want a way to make giving a family affair to transmit the values of being a benefactor to the next generation.

Sources of Donations to Nonprofits

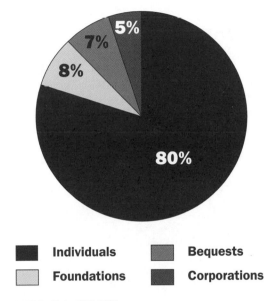

| Individuals | Bequests |
| Foundations | Corporations |

Source: AAFRC, Giving USA 1997

Top Foundations and Their Annual Giving (in millions)	
Ford Foundation	$348
Robert Wood Johnson Foundation	267
W.K. Kellogg Foundation	253
Pew Charitable Trusts	180
Lilly Endowment	167
J.D. & C.T. MacArthur Foundation	146
Atlantic Foundation and Trust	140
Andrew W. Mellon Foundation	114
Rockefeller Foundation	107
Annenberg Foundation	89

Source: The Foundation Center

Philanthropists like these people sincerely want to do good works. But just about everyone keeps an eye on the tax and estate planning aspects of philanthropy, too.

Seven Good Reasons for Charitable Giving

Let's look at the main reasons people cite for starting a foundation. These may be similar to yours, or may give you some new ideas. People establish foundations to. . .

Create the Perfect Legacy

A private foundation has often been called "the perfect legacy," because a foundation has permanence: it keeps going as long as the assets are wisely invested. Some foundations founded in the last century are still going strong.

"I like the idea of something going on and on, still being of value."- AJR

"As I got older, I thought more about what I wanted to be known for. The legacy idea became compelling." - SBG

And a foundation is a legacy, because it will keep supporting the causes you value. The documents you execute to create the foundation define its mission, which is whatever you choose it to be. If you want to focus on education, you create the foundation to do so. If you want to focus on the arts, you can do that too. Of course, you could leave that decision up to the trustees, but we find that most people have very clear ideas about what they want their foundation to do.

Many philanthropists think of a private foundation as a perfect legacy because it is truly a gift that keeps on giving back to the world. When we asked over 300 people how important this aspect was in their decision to create a private foundation, we found we struck a responsive chord. Over nine in ten founders of foundations (93%) said the idea of leaving a legacy was extremely important in their thinking.

Make a Better World

We find that affluent people are the most grateful people there are. Affluent people share a wonderment at how fortunate they are to be well off, and while they acknowledge the importance of hard work, they also simply feel lucky.

"I know I have been very lucky. Sure, I worked hard, but a lot of people do. In my case, it paid off. Now I want to give some of that back. I want to create opportunities for others, and help people the way I was helped as I came up. The foundation helps me do that." - HRD

"I was very fortunate growing up. I was helped by a number of people and that is why I am as successful as I am. I want to reach out to young people the way others reached out to me. That's why I started this program."- DBN

The Importance of Leaving a Legacy

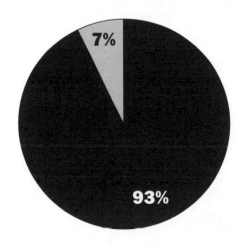

■ **Creating a legacy is extremely important**

□ **Creating a legacy is less important**

Source: Perfect Legacy Study, Prince & Associates

People who establish foundations have wonderful, exciting ideas about how to make a better world:

Julie and James live well today because the community helped make their business successful. They just established a private foundation to fund community cultural institutions. *"The community helped us build our business,"* confides

James, *"So we want to do what we can to make our community the best it can be. For us, that means giving real support to the institutions that we can all share - the theater, the symphony, the art museum."*

Saul is retired and now spends several months a year in Florida. Having a world-class medical facility helps everybody, and his foundation supports the hospital among other health and medical concerns. As Saul explains, *"Having a great hospital is something the community does together. I like being a part of that."*

People who establish foundations are idealists. Most of them (84%) say that the simple act of trying to make a better world was vital in their thinking when they set up a foundation.

The Importance of Making a Better World

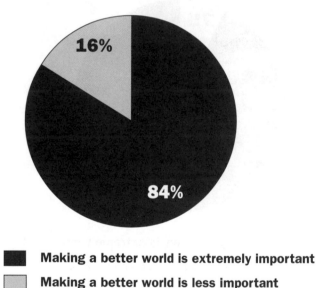

■ Making a better world is extremely important

□ Making a better world is less important

Source: Perfect Legacy Study, Prince & Associates

Actively Involve Family in Charitable Giving

Most philanthropically inclined families make giving a part of their everyday lives:

Ted Turner started the Turner Family Foundation in 1991. All five of his children are on the board, and they are active in deciding how to give away $25 million a year.

The Lilly Endowment was founded by Josiah K. Lilly, Sr., and his two sons. One son was Chairman of the Endowment, the other was responsible for day-to-day operations. Later on, a member of the third generation of the family also became involved.

Evelyn remembers how it was at her house, *"We just grew up with it. My parents were big in the local hospital and symphony, and they talked about their projects at dinner. Often the people who came to dinner were also involved. Talking about nonprofits was just a normal thing at our table."* Evelyn's foundation continues the tradition. Both her sons have joined her as trustees, and active support of charitable causes is still a central family concern.

The Importance of Involving the Family

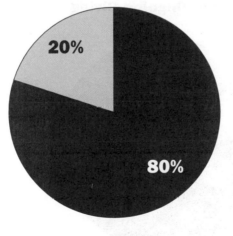

20%

80%

■ Involving the family is extremely important

▢ Involving the family is less important

Source: Perfect Legacy Study, Prince & Associates

Many of the people we know who have established foundations like bringing the family together in foundation-related activities:

Jim explains, *"It has given us a focus as a family, a way to feel good about what our family is and has done. Having my family together with me when we give away grants makes me feel good inside."* Alice adds, *"And I like what it says about our family. I like being a family that cares about the community and the world."*

Involving the family in charitable giving through a foundation is a widespread desire. Fully 80% of people setting up private foundations say the opportunity to involve their family in charitable giving was very important to them.

People also establish foundations to have...

The Joy of Sustained Giving

Many people who start private foundations have made major charitable gifts over the years. These gifts have been wonderful life events for many people. But many find that having a foundation is even more gratifying because they have the pleasure and satisfaction from making giving decisions on an ongoing basis.

The Importance of Ongoing Giving

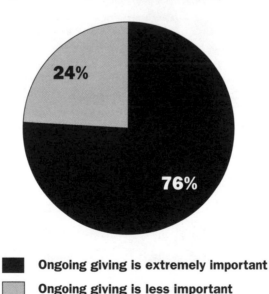

■ Ongoing giving is extremely important

□ Ongoing giving is less important

Source: Perfect Legacy Study, Prince & Associates

Since a foundation has to give away a certain amount every year (details on this later), grants have to be made on an annual basis.

"Before I created the foundation, I didn't realize how worthwhile it would be to me to see my programs grow year after year," says William.

Oscar and Betty like the fact that the causes they care most about will have an ongoing stream of support from them. *"These are things we care about very deeply. It means a lot to us to know they will always be taken care of."*

People who have recently set up foundations agree that the opportunity to do some ongoing giving is very important. Of the more than three hundred founders of foundations in the study, 76% said they found the chance to give on an ongoing basis very appealing.

The Ability to Change Your Mind

One of the great benefits of a private foundation is that you can change the focus of your giving as your interests change. Donors who set up charitable trusts usually make a one-time choice about the charity that will receive the gift. With a foundation, you make giving decisions every year. You can decide to concentrate on health causes one year and education the next.

The Importance of Flexibility in Giving

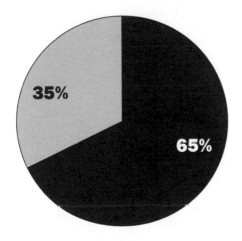

35%

65%

■ **Flexibility in giving is extremely important**

□ **Flexibility in giving is less important**

Source: Perfect Legacy Study, Prince & Associates

Foundations let your giving patterns change over time (within the parameters of your foundation's legal charter, which you, after all, set up). With the board of trustees, you can decide to support new charities, or you can stop giving to charities that are not performing efficiently.

"I like to support new programs being started by an institution. I support them for two or three years, and then move on. That way, they have to get on their own two feet, and my foundation can get involved with something new." - QRF

Private foundations are a key force in social, scientific and cultural innovation. The flexibility of a private foundation lets you change the direction of your giving so you can be a part of the important issues and events of our day, and affect the future in a positive way as well.

Flexibility in giving is important to people who establish foundations. In our research, we found that 65% of people who have established foundations in the past three years said that they liked the way foundations gave them the option to change or redirect their giving based on changing circumstances.

Tax and Estate Planning Benefits

Foundations can help in your tax and estate planning. Although this is rarely the most important reason to set up a foundation, tax and estate considerations can help in your decision making.

In terms of current tax planning, when you give a gift to your foundation you are able to take a tax deduction (subject to certain rules and regulations).

Foundations also help with estate planning. To take just one example, an estate is allowed to deduct the full amount used to fund a foundation that is set up under a will. Certainly, a good foundation feasibility study will address many estate planning issues. This is very important. If a major estate is unplanned, taxes can take as much as 65% of the total assets. With planning, the tax burden can be greatly reduced. The discipline required to set up a foundation will help you address significant estate planning issues as well.

Relatively few people (32%) say that these sorts of tax and estate planning advantages are extremely important to them when they think about why they set up a foundation. But people who set up foundations are sensitive to these issues; 68% say these issues are of some importance in their thinking.

The Importance of Tax and Estate Planning Advantages

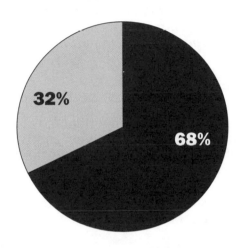

■ **Tax and estate planning advantages are somewhat important**

☐ **Tax and estate planning advantages are extremely important**

Source: Perfect Legacy Study, Prince & Associates

Organized Charitable Giving

A lot of the people we talk to like the way a private foundation helps them manage their giving.

"I don't have to feel guilty about not giving to every appeal that comes my way. I know I give a lot through the foundation, so it is easy to set aside all other requests," Anne explained to us one day. Her husband, Bill, sees it a little differently. *"What I didn't expect, but I like about having our foundation, is that I can refer people to the foundation. I am uncomfortable when people solicit me. Now, instead of having to say yes or no, I just tell them to give Dave a call over at the foundation."*

Having a foundation helps you become more effective and focused in your giving. Many people for whom we have done foundation feasibility studies are surprised at the amount they give to charity over the years. But they are even more surprised when they see how fragmented or scattered that giving is.

"I was giving a lot, but it was all over the map," Claire explains to people asking her advice. *"When we did the foundation feasibility study, I could see the difference between scattering around my giving and focusing it on one or two areas. The foundation has helped me pull my giving together, and I like that."*

Foundations and You

When you are thinking about an important move like creating a foundation, it's helpful to know how your motivations relate to those of other philanthropists. The idea of the Seven Faces of Philanthropy helps you to do so.

Whether or not you should have a private foundation can be answered by the seven good reasons for charitable giving:

- Create the Perfect Legacy

- Make a Better World

- Actively Involve Family in Charitable Giving

- The Joy of Sustained Giving

- The Ability to Change Your Mind

- Tax and Estate Planning Benefits

- Organized Charitable Giving

---

[1] All of this discussion is taken from the book The Seven Faces of Philanthropy written by two of us (Prince and File) published in 1994 by Jossey-Bass in San Francisco, CA. This framework was based on several years of research among hundreds of affluent (annual gifts exceeding $50,000) givers. The analytical methodology is based on psychographic segmentation.

Just What Is a Foundation?

> *"Wealth is nothing new in the history of the world. Nor is charity.*
> *But the idea of using private wealth imaginatively,*
> *constructively, and systematically to attack the fundamental problems*
> *of humankind is new."*
> *- John W. Gardner*

Just what is a foundation? Here's a fun definition from Dwight McDonald, who wrote *The Ford Foundation: The Men and the Millions:*

"A foundation is a large body of money completely surrounded by people who want some."

Here's a more formal, legalistic definition from the Foundation Center:

"A foundation is a nongovernmental, nonprofit organization with its own funds (usually from a single source, either an individual, family or corporation) and program managed by its own trustees and directors, which was established to maintain or aid educational, social, charitable, religious or other activities serving the common welfare primarily by making grants to other nonprofit organizations."

Defining a foundation in terms that make lawyers comfortable is actually very difficult because, legally, a foundation is what is left over after a lot of exemptions to 501(c)(3) organizations are listed.

For our purposes, a foundation is basically a simple concept: A foundation is a separate legal entity that has assets given to it by a single individual or family. It invests those assets and gives away grants, which are equivalent to 5% of its assets, to nonprofits each year. Its only tax obligation is an excise tax of 1 to 2%.

Think of it this way: You decide to create a foundation and fund it with $1,000,000. The foundation hires an investment firm to invest its assets, and the yield (after investment-related expenses) is 13% or $130,000.

Now the foundation looks at the expense side: The foundation must give away an amount equivalent to 5% of the assets, or about $50,000 (using $1,000,000 as the base). There is also the excise tax of 1 to 2%, or about $15,000. In addition there are administrative expenses of $20,000. Total expenses are $50,000 + $15,000 + $20,000 or $85,000. This leaves $25,000 that can be used in a couple of ways.

In years when the investment income exceeds expenses, the foundation has basically two choices: It can give away the extra $25,000 income to charities, or it can add the $25,000 to its asset base to enhance the foundation and to be a buffer in years when investment performance is poor.

Theoretically, foundations can last forever. If investment performance consistently earns enough to meet tax obligations and the rule about giving away an amount equal to at least 5% of assets, foundations can go on and on and on. Many famous foundations formed in the nineteenth century are stronger than ever. Even after as many as five generations, some foundations are still making significant contributions to American life. Just look at the Ford, Rockefeller, and Carnegie foundations.

This possibility of something that you create being around for a very long time is extremely appealing. Many people who establish foundations speak about them as though they were very precious, like their children.

"I have to be honest. I just really like the idea of something I started existing long after me. It gives me a great sense of still being around, caring about the things I care about." - FBC

"I guess I am pretty proud of what I have been able to do in the environmental area. I like the idea of knowing that some of what I think is important will be watched over for a long, long time." - DVT

Of course, if investment performance is consistently poor, the foundation will have to deplete its asset base in order to pay its taxes and give to charities. Over time, it may have to spend down the asset base and eventually disappear. Even then, however, it will have done a great deal of good.

There is an alternative to the type of foundation we have been discussing, and that is the operating foundation. An operating foundation is one that uses all its investment income to fund its own operations. The J. Paul Getty Trust is a good example. The Getty Trust does not make grants to other organizations. Instead, it supports its own research staff, laboratories and museums. Most people interested in foundations do not find that an operating foundation meets their needs.

Just What *Is* a Foundation?

Essentially, a foundation is a separate legal entity that gives away money to nonprofits. It makes its money by investing.

Alternatives to Private Foundations

"Founders of foundations are business people after all. They want to give their money away with the same intelligence and intensity that they applied to making their money."
- Peter Hero

A private foundation is not your only choice to achieve your charitable goals. There are alternatives that you and your advisor should carefully consider. One relatively new idea that has many of the same advantages as a private foundation is the supporting organization. Another alternative is the donor advised fund, which allows you the same control over giving with the efficiency of working within a community foundation. In addition, trusts have always been a useful alternative to consider.

These alternatives differ in how long they last. A trust, for example, can't last more than a couple of generations. A foundation could, conceivably, last forever (although this is unlikely). Supporting organizations offer tax and financial benefits over a trust, but are not suitable for every situation. You give up some control (especially over investment management) with most donor advised funds and trusts.

Type	How long it will last	Relative tax benefits	Relative level of personal control
Foundation	No limit	Moderate	Highest
Supporting Organization	No limit	Higher	Highest
Donor advised	No limit	Moderate	Moderate
Trust	A few generations	Highest	Moderate

Supporting Organizations

Supporting organizations are a new alternative to foundations. Like a foundation, they involve setting assets aside to benefit a charity (they have to be linked in approved ways with one or more existing public charities). They offer special advantages that foundations do not, under current rules. Contributions to a supporting organization receive a more favorable tax treatment, and a supporting organization is not subject to excise taxes. A supporting organization can also make better use of highly appreciated stock.

"I started off being sure a foundation was right for me. But I have a lot of company stock that has appreciated a great deal. When we looked at the alternatives up close, I found out a supporting organization was better for what I wanted to do."- NRB

Because the advantages and disadvantages are so complex, you should rely on a financial professional to do an analysis of the pros and cons for you, and show you the results in a foundation feasibility plan. Currently, few people (11%) seriously consider supporting organizations as an alternative to a foundation, but we find that more and more people are doing so.

Did You Evaluate Supporting Organizations as an Alternative to a Foundation?

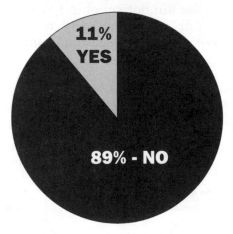

Source: Perfect Legacy Study, Prince & Associates

Donor Advised Funds

You could give the same amount of money to a community foundation and have them set it aside in a donor advised fund. This way the community foundation takes over the administrative and investment tasks, but you still select the charities and causes that will receive the donations. Again, there are many pros and cons, and a financial advisor can help you focus on the factors that affect your particular situation.

"I grew up in this community and our family business is in this town. Our workers, suppliers, and customers are here. I've spent my career working to make this town great, and so I really liked the idea of having a donor advised fund in a community foundation. I had been active in raising money for the foundation, so it was a good feeling to have our family be a part of it." - ISD

Did You Evaluate Donor Advised Funds as an Alternative to a Foundation?

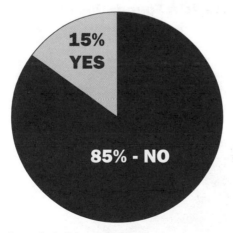

Source: Perfect Legacy Study, Prince & Associates

If you are like most Communitarians, you will find donor advised funds particularly appealing. Donor advised funds operating through community foundations tend to focus on the local area that is the target of the foundation. Most limit their giving to a particular town or region.

More and more people are evaluating donor advised funds (15%). As increasing numbers of people have foundation feasibility studies done, these alternatives to foundations will be more systematically and seriously considered.

Trusts

For years, trusts have been a key ingredient in financial and estate planning, and especially in charitable estate and financial planning. Trusts also offer tax and estate planning benefits. In addition, the people setting up the trust can be confident that the money is being used as they wish.

You could use trusts to accomplish your charitable objectives without ever setting up a foundation, or you could use trusts to fund your foundation. There are many ways to use trusts in these situations; which particular way is most appropriate depends on the circumstances. One of the benefits of a foundation feasibility study is that this issue will be explored for you.

Did You Evaluate Trusts as an Alternative to a Foundation?

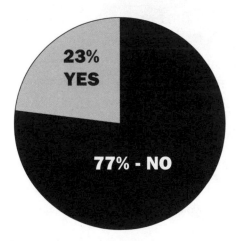

23%
YES

77% - NO

Source: Perfect Legacy Study, Prince & Associates

More people look at trusts when they are thinking of a private foundation than look at supporting organizations or donor advised funds. However, the number of people who consider trusts (23%) should be greater.

"I think of myself as pretty smart when it comes to business, and that's the way I approached this question. After looking at the situation in detail, I ended up going with a trust instead of a foundation because of the tax advantages." - LRC

Alternatives to Private Foundations

Before becoming committed to one course of action, you'll want to explore the pros and cons for your personal situation of these alternatives:

- Foundation

- Supporting organization

- Donor advised fund

- Trust

Should I Have a Private Foundation?

> *"Individuals may form communities, but it is institutions*
> *alone that can create a nation."*
> *- Benjamin Disraeli*

Foundations are not for everybody. By now, you may be wondering if a foundation is right for you. We've created a quick checklist you can use.

A Personal Checklist

Here is a quick checklist for you to gauge just how ready you are to create a private foundation.

Personal Readiness Checklist

Do you think about your legacy?	a. Not at all b. Once in a while c. A great deal
Do you know which charities you would like to support?	a. No b. Vaguely c. Yes
Are you willing to commit the time?	a. Already overextended b. Not much time c. Willing to invest the time
Can you afford it?	a. I'm fully invested now; don't want to move anything b. I don't want to do anything as major as $500,000 c. I was anticipating $500,000 or more

Scoring your results:

Give yourself   1 point for every "a,"
                       2 points for every "b" and
                       3 points for every "c."
Whatever your point total, keep reading the book.

9 to 12 points: You're Ready Now. You have all the characteristics of a founder of a private foundation. You have the assets at hand, are willing to commit the time, are clear about your goals, and want to involve your family.

6 to 8 points: Look But Don't Leap. You are interested in establishing a private foundation, but there are some major obstacles in your way. Either your assets aren't very transferable right now, or you are overcommitted in other areas. You may want to start a few low-key foundation-related initiatives but not swing into high gear until the time is right.

4 to 6 points: Not This Year. You might be interested in a private foundation but have a lot of questions and reservations.

The checklist touched on issues important to consider. Here is a more in-depth discussion of those issues:

Do You Think About Your Legacy?

People who establish private foundations have typically been thinking about their legacy for some time. Often in the prime of life, they have a lot of achievements behind them. They begin to think about what they would like to do, or leave behind, or be known for.

"I've been active in this area for many years as an attorney. I've been involved in a lot of the development that has been done around here. Making more money does not interest me that much. I've been thinking what I want to leave behind." - VRB

"I think a man gets to a certain age and begins to think more long-term. The kids are grown, he's well established... it's time for him to consider what he wants to be known for." - SDA

William Hewlett had served on the grant-making committee of the San Francisco Foundation for many years before he set up his own private foundation. When it came time to establish his foundation, he knew exactly which causes he wanted to support. An avid outdoorsman, he was very interested in environmental issues, and that became a major focus of his foundation.

Do You Know Which Philanthropies You Would Like to Support?

We find that most people who create a private foundation have been donors, often big donors, for a long time. They are experienced philanthropists (although most would be too modest to call themselves philanthropists). They know what they like to give to, and how they want to relate to nonprofits. Quite often, their private foundation is an extension of many years of giving.

Ted Turner's Turner Family Foundation gives to causes that share a commitment to global issues such as the environment and children's welfare. Through the first three quarters of 1997, the Turner Family Foundation allocated its gifts among habitat and the environment, population, clean water, and energy as shown in the table below. Typical recipients include the Smithsonian, Bat Conservation International, Planned Parenthood, Greenpeace Russia, and the Rocky Mountain Institute.

Turner Family Foundation Philanthropic Support

Environment	$5,486,000
Population	2,530,000
Clean water	1,818,000
Energy	1,729,000
Other	1,395,000

Source: Turner Family Foundation, Newsweek

Elise and Ken have been active in giving to cancer causes and in raising money for cancer causes for years. Both have had family members stricken by the disease, and they worry about their children's genetic inheritance. When Ken started to think about retirement, they decided to look at a foundation. In their case, they knew what they wanted to support.

Bruce and Kathy were quite clear about their objectives, too.

They had enjoyed collecting art over the years, and planned to give their collections to several museums. Mindful of the burden this would place on the museums, they decided that a foundation would be the perfect way for them to keep on supporting art museums.

Americans support a wide range of causes:

Allocation of Individual Donations

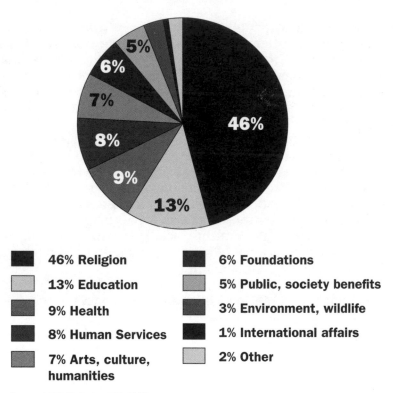

	46% Religion		6% Foundations
	13% Education		5% Public, society benefits
	9% Health		3% Environment, wildlife
	8% Human Services		1% International affairs
	7% Arts, culture, humanities		2% Other

Source: AAFRC, Giving USA 1997

Are You Willing to Commit the Time?

Like everything, a foundation can take up a lot or a little time, depending on how you organize it. If you invite grants, someone has to read and evaluate them. If you give to specific programs, you have to be prepared to evaluate the effectiveness of your support. You can choose to have many and long meetings of the board of trustees, or few and efficient ones. You can do some administration yourself, or you can outsource that work.

Percent of Foundations Supporting Each Area

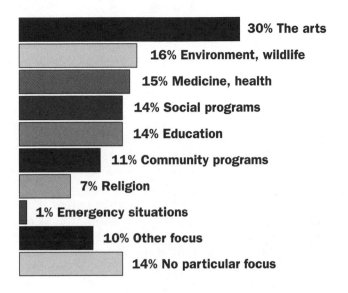

Source: Perfect Legacy Study, Prince & Associates

What is a realistic time budget? Let's assume you do as most do, and outsource the administration (record keeping, tax documents, etc.) and have an independent asset manager. Let's also assume you want to be involved in the decisions about who will be getting the grants. If your board of trustees does not invite grant proposals, but gives to institutions you know well, you could be talking about just one meeting a year.

Certainly, you could cut the time commitment to zero by not being on the board of trustees, but we rarely see this done. Most people who set up a private foundation like being involved.

We find that most people like quarterly meetings of the foundation's board of trustees. This is often enough to create a good feeling of involvement, but not so often it becomes burdensome.

Do You Feel It's Important to Involve Your Family in Philanthropic Activities?

To many people, teaching their children about giving is an important priority and responsibility. Andrew Carnegie actually wrote a book saying that the "responsibility of wealth" is charitable giving and that, through one's own example, one should inspire others to do the same.

"My family went through some good times and some hard times. But even in the hard times, there was always enough to give to others. It was something I grew up with, and it is something I have tried to pass along to my children." - JHT

"From the time my children were seven, I have been bringing them along to charities. When my children got an allowance, I had them set aside a little for charity. I felt it was important to establish these principles at a young age." - FRC

One of the major advantages of a foundation is that it can be a family affair. Just about everyone starting a foundation brings their family into it as trustees. This way the family comes together in a special way at special times to talk about how to help others. As the children get older, having a foundation is one more way to bring the family together.

"I found my children really liked the idea of the foundation when I spoke to them about it. They said, 'Dad, we know your school has been very important to you through the years. We can't think of a better thing for you to do.' And so we created a foundation focused on education. We get together once a year to formally decide on our giving decisions, but we talk about foundation-related issues all the time." - ANS

"It seems as though the family is spinning apart. Everybody has their own priorities and we live further apart than we used to. I like the foundation as a family idea, something the family stands for and continues to share, no matter how far apart we become." - MCR

Because foundations can exist though many generations, we find that many of them are named after the founding families, such as the Pew Charitable Trust (which is really a foundation in spite of its name) or the Robinson Family Foundation. This way, a legacy is started for the family as a whole.

Can You Afford It?

Here is the short answer: Yes.

We have helped people set up foundations for as little as $100,000. Of course, there are also foundations with $100 million or more in assets.

Many people think they can't afford a foundation until someone explains to them how they can. In fact, only 5% of the people who recently set up a foundation thought they could before doing the analysis. The remaining 95% thought they didn't have the assets to set up a foundation when, in fact, they did. If someone hadn't explained it to them, they would have missed the opportunity simply because they didn't know it existed.

Did You Think You Could Set Up a Foundation Before a Financial Advisor Showed You How it was Possible?

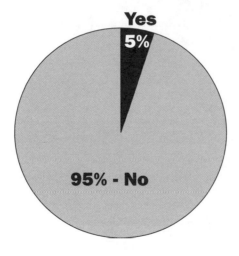

Source: Perfect Legacy Study, Prince & Associates

One benchmark used by a lot of people is that a minimum of $25,000 should be available every year for giving away as grants to charities. That would be a foundation of about $750,000 (which will also give you a cushion for fees and other expenses).

Unless a foundation is well funded, it will not generate enough income from investments to make substantial giving possible each year after administrative costs are covered. On the other hand, there are ways to build up the foundation assets over time and ways to keep administrative costs down.

To give you some perspective, consider the breakdown in size of over 300 foundations that were set up in the past three years. One in ten is smaller than $3 million, and most are in the $3 to $5 million range. You should also note that this is the projected size of the foundation when it is fully funded, which quite often does not happen immediately. Most people transfer assets to a foundation over time; others fully fund the foundation through a trust or life insurance as part of their estate. When you set up your foundation, you usually have a plan for fully funding the foundation, and a target amount in mind.

Foundation Size (When Fully Funded)

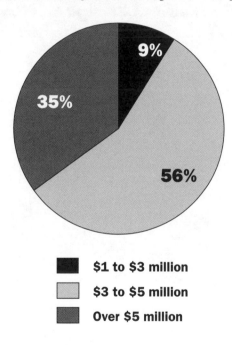

■ $1 to $3 million
□ $3 to $5 million
■ Over $5 million

Source: Perfect Legacy Study, Prince & Associates

Should I Have a Private Foundation?

Should you have a private foundation? It depends on your answers to the personal checklist questions:

- Do you think about your legacy?

- Do you know which charities you would like to support?

- Are you willing to commit the time?

- Do you feel it's important to involve your family in philanthropic activities?

- Can you afford it?

How to Set Up Your Private Foundation

"Foundations are the lengthened shadows of a few individuals."
- Waldemar A. Nelson

So, you have made a tentative decision to go ahead with a foundation.

What's next?

Frankly, the hard work of planning and implementing is what's next. Like a lot of things worth doing, setting up a foundation can be complex. You need to be sure it is done right, so there are no tax or estate difficulties down the road. You can, and should, retain experts to guide you through the legal, financial, and regulatory mazes. But the only one who can, in the end, make the decisions is you.

> Only you can truly decide on what you want your legacy to be.

> Only you can decide on the nature of family involvement and build interest in the foundation among family members.

> Only you can authorize a foundation feasibility study and have it done.

> Only you can start the sequence that will result in the final implementation of your foundation.

The sections that follow are a step-by-step process for actually setting up a foundation. However, unlike other books on the subject, we will not go into a lot of technical detail. We will focus on the experiences of others who have set up foundations, so that you can build on their successes.

Deciding on Your Legacy

Most foundations have a focus, or a set of particular causes, they like to fund. As the founder of the foundation, your wishes here are the most important, and the foundation documents can (and should) specify the mission of the foundation.

Foundations are almost limitless in their possibilities. Alfred Nobel established a foundation to honor the very best people in several fields; his foundation now administers and awards the Nobel prizes. Due to the good investment management of the foundation, an average Nobel prize is now worth over $1 million to the winner. There are now many different foundations that reward achievement in different fields through prizes, such as the Pritzkers in medicine and the Pulitzers in journalism.

The MacArthurs were concerned that there was not enough support given to the talented person who had not yet achieved fame. Their foundation was established to identify and award prizes to people of particular promise. The result is the so-called "genius grants" that get so much publicity.

George Soros made his money in investments in America after his family emigrated from Eastern Europe. His foundation now supports educational and market reform in that part of the world with "Open Society" grants. Grants to Russia through his foundation are expected to exceed $500 million. He is committed to doing what he can to help the area develop.

The Nortons are contemporary art collectors. They observed that it is more difficult for art museum curators to mount a show of contemporary art than the more familiar and popular schools of art. To fill this gap, they established a foundation to give grants to curators interested in mounting these "riskier" contemporary art exhibits.

Here are a few more examples. Henry Kaiser focused his foundation on pre-paid health plans. His interest in health care was shared by Robert Wood Johnson. Richard King Mellon was most interested in urban redevelopment, while Paul Mellon cared most about the humanities. Rockefeller set up his foundation to focus on the causes of social ills.

Of course, it is possible to evolve your ideas, as Will Kellogg did when he established the W. K. Kellogg Foundation at the age of 65. His first commitment was to helping handicapped children. Upon further reflection, he decided that the necessities of food, health, and clothing were essential to all children, and so he broadened his commitment to address those needs as well. Thinking further, he decided that poverty is a result of an insufficient education, and so he broadened his foundation's scope still further to focus on the education of the poor.

As you can see, the focus of a private foundation is limited only by your imagination. (Of course, it is also limited by the fact that those who receive your grants must be legally charitable organizations).

Deciding on the Nature of Family Involvement

Once you have a sense of the general focus of your foundation, you can think about what kind of family involvement you would like. The usual way is to include your children with you on the board. Of course, it is important to be sure the children want this involvement, so it is good to talk it through with them as you work through the process of setting up your foundation. That's why we suggest that you do this step now, instead of after all the rest of the work on the foundation is done.

Did You Have a Foundation Feasability Study Done?

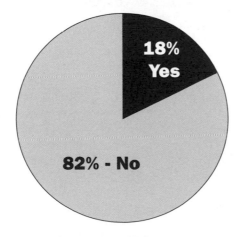

Source: Perfect Legacy Study, Prince & Associates

Your children will want to know what is expected of them. While you will know more specifics after your foundation feasibility study is done, you can generally tell them that they should expect to join the family for at least one foundation meeting per year (expenses borne by the foundation), and to receive periodic reports and communications in between.

Getting a Foundation Feasibility Study Done

This is an essential step. A good foundation feasibility study will lay out your options and choices. Although the advisability of a foundation feasibility study seems obvious, not everyone has them done. In fact, in our study of over 300 people who recently set up foundations, just 18% had a formal plan completed.

Looking Back, Would You Have Liked a Foundation Feasability Study Done?

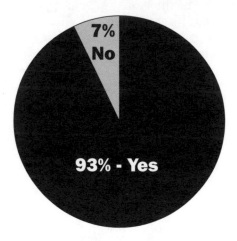

7%
No

93% - Yes

Source: Perfect Legacy Study, Prince & Associates

However, having been through the process, they all agree (93%) that a foundation feasibility study would have been a good thing to have done.

"It got pretty complicated at points. I'd have liked some sort of road map going in." - LNH

"Even though I'm well acquainted with my financial portfolio, I felt reassured once I had a feasibility study done. It was beneficial to have my instincts confirmed." - JSW

If the foundation were not reason enough for having a feasibility study done, your estate plan is. Unfortunately, all too many people don't keep their estate plans updated — just look at the next chart. Not many more than one in ten have a fully up-to-date estate plan, while 42% have an estate plan that was reviewed recently. A foundation feasibility study is a good excuse for another look. But if you happen to be among the 22% with on older estate plan (one not updated in the past five years) or even among the 23% without an adequate estate plan, a financial feasibility study is exactly what you need.

Current Status of Estate Plans

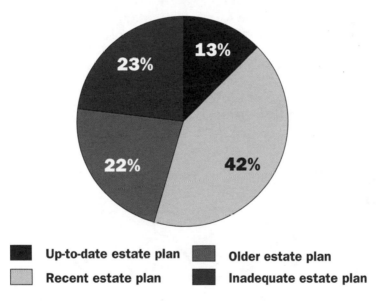

Source: *Perfect Legacy Study, Prince & Associates*

Financial Aspects of a Foundation Feasibility Study

The first major component of the foundation feasibility study is the size of the foundation. You'll want to review all your goals (trusts for the family, insuring successful business transition, etc.) in order to decide on the proportion of your assets you want to place in the foundation. One of the chief benefits of a foundation feasibility study is that your advisor can show you ways to fund a foundation you may not have thought of. For example, you can fund a foundation through your estate, or over time or through life insurance. The case studies in Chapter Six show you some of the different ways you may want to consider.

The second major component is the selection of which assets to transfer because of their basis value. That is one of the reasons to have a foundation feasibility study.

Russ Prince likes to say that affluent people have only one choice, and that choice is whether to be philanthropic on a voluntary or involuntary basis. The chart below paints the picture (only slightly overstated for illustrative purposes). Without an adequate estate plan, most people will wind up only being able to pass on an average of 50% to their heirs, with the rest going to the IRS in the form of "involuntary philanthropy." With an adequate estate plan, however, people are able to pass the same 50% to heirs, but the other 50% can be redirected to the charities they prefer.

A Comparison of Voluntary and Involuntary Philanthropy

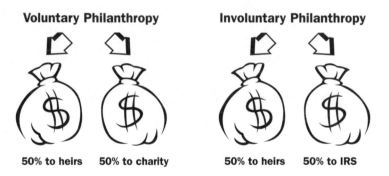

Private foundations are not as tax-advantaged as other forms of charitable giving (particularly trusts), but they have all the other advantages we have discussed. Private foundations do, however, receive some favorable tax treatment. You will want to check these out with your advisor, as new rules and regulations may change these, but the main tax-related advantages are:

- Donors can take a deduction of up to 30% of their adjusted gross income in any year.

- Publicly traded stock may be deducted at full fair market value (not the original basis) within some limits, and only up to 20% of the donor's adjusted gross income.

- Other property (such as closely-held stock and real estate) may be deducted at cost up to a value equivalent to 20% of the donor's adjusted gross income.

- Bequests are deducted from the estate at full value.

A foundation feasibility study also gives you a number of options for the financial structure of your foundation. You will decide on the shape of your foundation when you and your advisor work through the details based on your personal situation.

Implementing Your Foundation

Once you have decided on your mission and the shape of the foundation, implementation is straightforward.

Creating the Legal Documents

If you are like most people, you have come to rely on your attorney over the years. Most likely, your attorney has been an active sounding board for you in your consideration of a private foundation. It is now time to rely on your attorney for creating the legal documents.

The required legal documents are called "the governing instruments of the foundation."

The two basic forms for a private foundation are a trust and a corporation. The advantages and disadvantages of these are a function of laws in the different states, so your attorney will have to help you sort through which structure would be better suited to your situation. In general, a corporation is more flexible, because of the greater latitude directors have (as opposed to trustees). If you are setting up a trust, the document will be your trust instrument. If you are setting up a corporation, you will have the articles of incorporation (or charter) and bylaws.

Since a private foundation is a legal entity, setting one up is an extensive legal process that has to be done right in order to get the tax exemption on the earnings of the assets under management. You must apply for tax status determination with the Internal Revenue Service within 15 months after creating your foundation, and state filings have to be done on a timely basis.

Who Administers the Foundation?

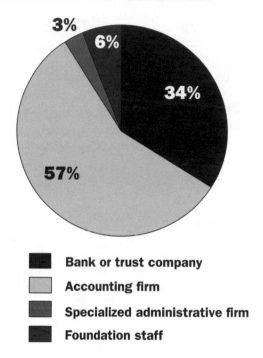

Bank or trust company

Accounting firm

Specialized administrative firm

Foundation staff

Source: Perfect Legacy Study, Prince & Associates

Selecting an Administrator

Due to all the legal requirements, a foundation generates a fair amount of administrative work. There are several ways to handle this. A few highly committed people have taken on this responsibility themselves. Bill Hewlett (co-founder of the Hewlett-Packard corporation) did so when he first established his foundation with $20 million. He personally made all the grant decisions and did all the administration with the help of his personal secretary. Eli Lilly said that he operated the Lilly Endowment out of the left-hand side of his desk for years.

Such a hands-on approach isn't for everybody. Even smaller foundations can find it efficient to outsource the administrative function. Bank trust companies or attorney's offices are resources to consider. Depending on the size of the foundation, it can be cost-effective to hire full-time administration staff.

Putting Together Your Board

Once your foundation is nearly operational, you should select your board of trustees. We find that people turn to people they have known and trusted over a long period of time to serve as trustees. Family members can certainly be involved. So, too, can longtime friends.

Members of Boards of Trustees

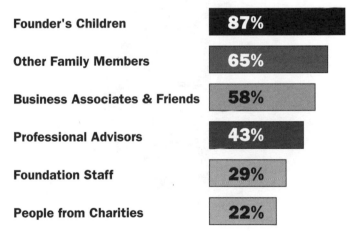

Founder's Children	87%
Other Family Members	65%
Business Associates & Friends	58%
Professional Advisors	43%
Foundation Staff	29%
People from Charities	22%

Source: Perfect Legacy Study, Prince & Associates

Bringing people you know and trust into the foundation circle is a practice among large as well as small foundations. When John MacArthur set up the John D. and Catherine T. MacArthur Foundation, he asked people he knew well to serve on his board. In addition to his wife, Catherine, and his son, J. Roderick, he turned to old business associates. These were three senior managers of his company and a radio personality who had long been sponsored by his company. Bill Hewlett also turned to his family when he sought to broaden his foundation. He involved his wife and their five children and also turned to the head of a community foundation he had known for a long time.

You will want to think ahead to the way future members will be selected. When you create the legal documents for the foundation, you will be able to specify the type of people you want to serve on the board. This will insure that your wishes are carried out over the long term. For example, you can specify what type of qualifications you'd like for your board members. You could require that they be active in certain other organizations, or have certain professional qualifications or a certain education, or a certain relationship to your family. J. D. and Cissy wanted people on their board who shared their commitment to the environment, so they specified that all future board members (even family members) should have a record of at least five years involvement with environmental causes.

Are You a Trustee of Your Own Foundation?

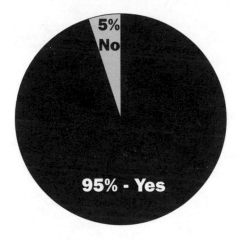

Source: Perfect Legacy Study, Prince & Associates

Later on, you could have current board members select new members who qualify according to the standards you set up. Or, you could provide that a panel of the presidents of the nonprofit organizations who are beneficiaries of your foundation name your board members. In this way, new members would be sure to be familiar with the institutions your foundation was set up to benefit.

Still another alternative is to have your descendents select new board members.

Of course, you will have to decide whether you want to sit on your foundation's board of trustees. You probably will, because that is where many people get a lot of their gratification. You won't be alone — just about everyone who sets up a private foundation chooses to join the board of trustees.

Selecting an Investment Advisor

One of your first actions will be to fund the foundation by transferring assets. Under current law and regulations, you do not have to transfer all your assets immediately. You can establish the foundation and schedule incremental transfers of funds as they become available. You can also fund the foundation through a trust or life insurance through your estate. The foundation can, of course, accept gifts from others, and family members may want to participate in this way.

Once you have begun the process of transferring assets to your foundation, you will want to select an investment manager for the foundation. There are a number of choices. You could go with a bank or trust company (as 28% do), or a financial advisor (as 27% do), or an investment management firm (as 26% do), or a brokerage firm (as 22% do). Some foundations use more than one type of investment manager, which is why these numbers add to more than 100%. In some cases (12%), the foundation staff manages the investment portfolio, but these are the very largest foundations where it is efficient to do so.

Who Handles the Investment Management Aspects of Your Foundation? (multiple answers)

Bank or Trust Company	28%
Financial Advisor	27%
Investment Management Firm	26%
Brokerage Firm	22%
Funds Managed by Foundation Staff	12%

Source: Perfect Legacy Study, Prince & Associates

In most cases, the person who is selected to manage the investment portfolio of the foundation is the same person who helped set up the foundation. That is, the analytic work of helping someone set up a foundation calls for a lot of tax- and financial-planning expertise. This same expertise is called for in managing the investment portfolio of a foundation. Most people find that the person who does the foundation feasibility study is usually a good candidate to manage the foundation's assets. Most people (71%) go with that person or firm.

"I'd always had Jim manage some of my portfolio, so when he approached me with the idea of a foundation, I was confident he could work with me on the issues. It took us more than a year to do all the thinking on the foundation. When it came time to decide on the investment advisor, I couldn't think of anyone better than Jim. He knew exactly what I was trying to achieve." - LRM

Transferring Assets

At this point, you will want to begin to implement the asset-transfer strategy you selected as part of your foundation feasibility study. As we have explained, there are many funding scheduling options, and you will decide on the one that best fits your needs as a result of the foundation feasibility study. Most recently established foundations will be between $3 and $5 million when they are fully funded.

Beginning the Work of Your Foundation

If you have decided to create a corporation, your board members will formally elect directors or officers and adopt bylaws at their first meeting. Regardless of the structure you have chosen, consider creating committees. Many foundations find at least four committees useful: an executive committee, an investment committee, a grants committee, and an audit committee.

Plan the next year's activities, including how many times to meet. Your meeting schedule will depend on a number of factors, such as the number of decisions you have to make and people's availability. Most people (57%) find that annual meetings work very well, but some meet more often.

How Often Does Your Foundation Meet?

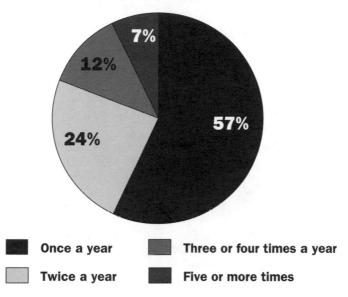

7%

12%

24%

57%

■ Once a year   ■ Three or four times a year

□ Twice a year   ■ Five or more times

Source: Perfect Legacy Study, Prince & Associates

Covering expenses and compensating trustees is a matter for foundations to individually decide. Some cover expenses and also pay trustees, regardless of whether or not they are a family member. Trustee fees currently average $5,000 a year with a small stipend per meeting. However, most private foundations do not provide any compensation to trustees (the family feels it is better to direct as much foundation money as possible to charities). Some foundations compromise and provide compensation to outside trustees but not to family members.

Many foundations find it useful to create a vision and mission statement, and lay out specific goals and objectives. Your board should also look ahead to initial funding levels.

It is also time to create grant-making policies and procedures. You don't have to accept grant applications or proposals unless you want to. In fact, most recently established foundations do not; a committee of all or part of the board decides to whom and toward what they give money.

How Do You Handle Decisions About Giving?

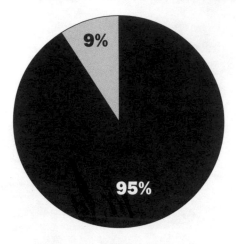

■ **We do not accept grant proposals;**
we make decisions

□ **We ask for grant proposals**

Source: Perfect Legacy Study, Prince & Associates

Obeying the Rules of the Road

Unfortunately, there have been abuses of private foundations, and there are now a number of rules and regulations to be aware of. A congressional investigation in the 1960's found that some private foundations had been set up in such a way as to directly benefit the founders and their families. In some cases, family members received grants from the foundation, or received low- or no-cost loans. In other cases, the foundation was endowed with art work or other assets that remained in the founder's home. As a result of the tax reform act of 1969 (and subsequent tax reform acts), a series of provisions were enacted to reduce the abuse possible through foundations.

Essentially, the principle is that a foundation should be an arm's length entity that exists for the support of charities. Some of the specific rules are called "rules against self-dealing," and these rules include:

- The founders and their family may not receive or use
  the income of the foundation.

- The founders and their family may not receive a loan from the foundation.

- The founders and their family many not keep assets of the foundation (e.g. art or antiques) on their premises.

However, you may pay for reasonable expenses incurred by the family in relation to foundation activities, and you may pay reasonable compensation (say, for serving as a trustee or being on the board) to family members. The key test is reasonable . Your advisors can brief you on the legal specifics that might pertain to your situation.

Another set of regulations stipulates that the foundation's assets be invested appropriately. So-called "jeopardy investments" are deemed too risky for a foundation because they place the interests of the prospective charities in danger. Jeopardy investments include highly speculative investments and futures. Foundations that invest prudently have no trouble.

You should also be aware that the tax returns of private foundations must be available for public inspection.

It's a good idea to spend some time with your advisor discussing how each of these rules applies to your personal situation so that you can be sure a private foundation will meet all your needs. Unfortunately, too few people do. In our research, we found that advisors did not explain the self-dealing, risky investment or company ownership limitations to more than half of the people who recently set up foundations. Many people were unaware about excise tax issues until after their foundations were already established. Just about the only rule everyone was aware of was the requirement to distribute income (equal to 5% of assets) to charities.

Carrying on Your Legacy

As you implement your foundation, be sure to think of ways that will enable the future managers of the foundation to stay true to your legacy. You may specify that family members involved in the foundation meet once a year to discuss your legacy and ways of being faithful to it. You can create documents explaining your thoughts, goals, and dreams.

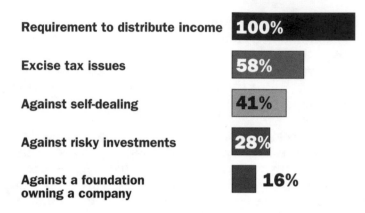

Percent Who Feel Their Financial Advisors Were Especially Helpful in Explaining the Following Regulations About Foundations

Requirement to distribute income **100%**

Excise tax issues **58%**

Against self-dealing **41%**

Against risky investments **28%**

Against a foundation owning a company **16%**

Source: Perfect Legacy Study, Prince & Associates

You want to be careful not to specify your foundation's goal in too much detail in the legal documents — you need to give later trustees some latitude to do the right thing if circumstances change. The Barnes Foundation ran into trouble in just this way.

The Barnes Foundation was set up just outside Philadelphia to house and care for Mr. Barnes' superb collection of Impressionist paintings and make them available to the public as a museum. Barnes loved his collection so much he specified in his foundation documents that every painting had to hang in just the spot he placed it, and that the collection could never travel. Well, over the years, the costs of running the museum exceeded the assets that were set aside in the foundation. A convenient solution was suggested: raise money to repair the museum and increase the foundation's assets by letting the seldom-seen paintings travel to other museums as a blockbuster show. The only problem was that this suggestion violated the letter of the foundation documents. After a heated public debate (and a court case) this was done. How much simpler it would have been had Mr. Barnes foreseen the need to give his future board members some latitude.

There are many creative ways to ensure that your current and future board members know and appreciate your vision. A popular way these days is to use a video tape. Another is to have prospective board members sit in on board meetings for a period of time before they assume their duties. In this way they become familiar with the vision of the foundation as well as the inner working of the board. The key is to build in regular and in-depth opportunities for the board and your family to review your original vision.

Now That the Foundation is Established, I Have Recommended Private Foundations to Others

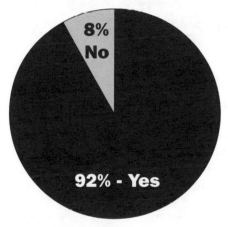

8%
No

92% - Yes

Source: Perfect Legacy Study, Prince & Associates

Enjoying Your Legacy

As you are all too aware, achieving financial success carries with it the burden of having to work through the many rules and regulations governing wealth in this country. Having done that, and having established your foundation, you now are in a position to enjoy the rewards of your legacy.

The exciting thing is that people who have set up foundations enjoy them mightily. Nearly everyone who has established a private foundation (92%) recommends them to others, and just about as many people (86%) say that now that the foundation is established, giving becomes more and more gratifying.

Now That the Foundation is Established, Giving Becomes More and More Gratifying

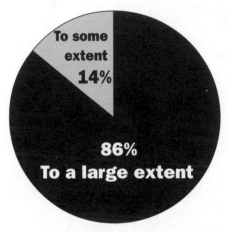

To some extent 14%

86% To a large extent

Source: Perfect Legacy Study, Prince & Associates

Even people heavily involved in charitable giving find that they become even more involved after they have the foundation. Many people who recently set up a foundation found that their involvement increased to a great extent (82%), and others found it went up at least a bit. People are happy with their new involvement.

"Before, I just gave a bit here and a bit there. Now, with the foundation, I find I think about things so much more. I have to figure out how to make the most of what we have to work with, and which organizations will be the most effective. I'm much more involved, but I've got to say that I'm loving every minute of it." - EJY

One significant mark of satisfaction is when you recommend your advisors to someone else. People who set up foundations are generally so satisfied (71%) that they have already recommended their foundation advisors to their friends and business associates.

Now That the Foundation is Established, I am More Involved with Charitable Giving

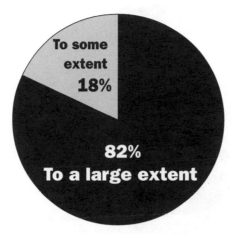

Source: Perfect Legacy Study, Prince & Associates

"Well, it's a natural thing, I suppose. Someone will ask about the foundation, and I will talk about what fun we are having with it. Then they'll ask how I figured out how to do it, and I'll explain our process and tell them about Mary. Next thing you know, I'm giving out Mary's telephone number. But I'm glad to do it, because she did a good job for us." - GCP

One of the burdens of wealth is that you are frequently asked to support some cause or another. Even the wealthiest person can't support everything he or she is asked to. People who establish foundations say that they find they are able to politely turn down requests for support by mentioning that all of their giving is channeled through their foundation now, and that decisions are no longer up to them but are made by a board of trustees.

"I can't tell you what a relief it is when people find out I have this foundation. Of course, I got used to all the asking, and had my little ways of dealing with it, but I have been amazed at how infrequently I am asked now that people know about the foundation." - TDS

Now That the Foundation is Established, I Have Recommended My Financial Advisor to Others

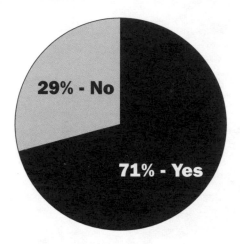

29% - No

71% - Yes

Source: Perfect Legacy Study, Prince & Associates

Many people who recently set up a foundation say that this has been a great benefit. Some 79% say that they feel substantially less barraged by solicitations from fund-raisers, and the rest (21%) say that they feel the foundation does protect them to some extent.

One of the most gratifying findings from our studies has been that people who start foundations say that they really do bring the family together in a shared purpose. A large proportion (62%) say their family is closer than ever before because of the shared interest in the foundation. A foundation is a larger-than-life goal the family can all share in and be proud of. It can emerge as part of the family identity, as the way family members feel good about being part of that family.

"I have to say I was surprised at how well the family came together. Like a lot of families, we have our differences. But we all value music. Starting a foundation focused on music education got a lot of us talking about what we could do, and I am very proud every time I see my family foundation listed in a concert program." - AMW

Now That the Foundation is Established, I Feel Less Barraged by Solicitations from Charities

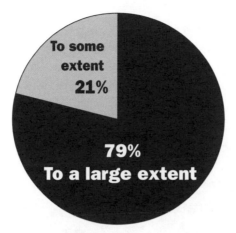

Source: Perfect Legacy Study, Prince & Associates

Now That the Foundation is Established, My Family is Closer Than Ever Before

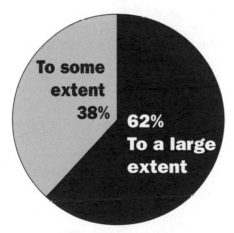

Source: Perfect Legacy Study, Prince & Associates

Just about everyone says that their foundation has been successful in drawing the family together. Of course, this will depend on the number of meetings you have every year (remember, the average is one), and how active your committees are. But 38% say that the foundation provides many more opportunities for family get-togethers, and the other 62% say that the foundation has been a positive force.

Now That the Foundation is Established, It Provides Opprotunities for the Family to Get Together

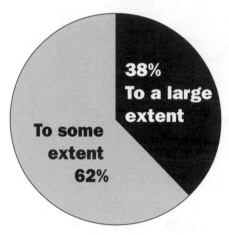

38%
To a large extent

To some extent 62%

Source: Perfect Legacy Study, Prince & Associates

Few people find the burdens and responsibilities of having a private foundation to be onerous. Most people (69%) say that the time commitment is not at all difficult to manage. Some say it is somewhat more than they expected (21%), and just a few (10%) say that the time commitment is just too much. Again, you can control this by the decisions you make. Decide to accept grant proposals and do your own administrative work if you want to give big time commitments. Do not accept proposals and hire others for administrative and investment management tasks, and your time commitment will be light. You can also make decisions to put in more or less time as your personal situation changes. The key here is planning.

We have met with founders who are overwhelmed by the administrative burden of running a foundation. We work with them to look for alternatives — turning some over to other family members, developing volunteer support, hiring staff part- or full-time, or retaining an accounting firm or bank to do administrative tasks.

Administrative tasks include organizing the giving. It also includes keeping track of gifts, expenses and income. It can include monitoring the gifts to the charity to be sure they are properly used.

Now That the Foundation is Established, I Find the Time Commitment Too Much

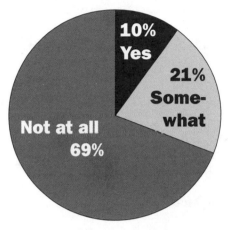

Source: Perfect Legacy Study, Prince & Associates

Now That the Foundation is Established, I Find the Administrative Burden Too Much

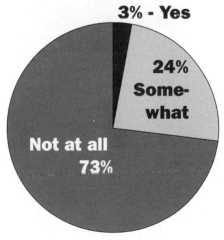

Source: Perfect Legacy Study, Prince & Associates

However, most people do not get into this bind. The great majority (73%) say that they to not find administrative tasks to be too difficult or time consuming. Some find that they need to do a little better planning (24%) and just a few (3%) are bothered by the amount of administrative work they find they need to do.

How to Set Up Your Private Foundation

There are so many people setting up foundations these days that the actual process is pretty straightforward. There are these four major steps:

- Deciding on Your Legacy

- Deciding on the Nature of Family Involvement

- Getting a Foundation Feasibility Study Done

- Implementing Your Foundation

Of these, the last planning step is getting the foundation feasibility study done. The last step is beginning the actual implementation. At this point, many more people become involved, and the foundation begins to take on a life of its own. The seven implementation steps include:

- Creating the Legal Documents

- Selecting an Administrator

- Putting Together Your Board

- Selecting an Investment Advisor

- Transferring Assets

- Beginning the Work of Your Foundation

- Obeying the Rules of the Road

- Carrying on Your Legacy

- Enjoying Your Legacy

Case Studies How Four Families Established Their Own Private Foundations

"Riches without charity are nothing worth. They are blessings only to him who makes them a blessing to others."
- Henry Fielding

There are many variations within the rules of setting up a private foundation; most variations revolve around the question of how the foundation will be funded. Four methods often used to fund a foundation are highly appreciated stock, a charitable remainder trust, life insurance, and annual contributions. The following case studies illustrate each of these four methods.

As you read through the studies, keep in mind that your own funding decision will be a personal choice based on your own circumstances. Note the similarities and differences between your own situation and the situations depicted in these studies, and notice how the decisions in these studies follow the framework laid out in Chapter 5.

Case Study #1

The Olson Family Foundation: Funding a Foundation by Using Highly Appreciated Stock

Mary and Tim Olson are both fifty-five years-of-age. Their three grown children have established their own lives and families in nearby states. Tim has worked for the same corporation for twenty-seven years; he now has a very senior position and his income is $500,000 a year. Mary is an active volunteer in their church and in community youth programs.

Deciding on the Legacy

One day in April, Mary and Tim sat down with Drew, their attorney, to review their estate plan. Drew wanted to know if there had been any big changes since they last met.

"Well, I'm thinking of retiring in five years," said Tim. *"I want to develop a successor for my position and make sure there's a successful transition, then retire — do some traveling Mary and I have long wanted to do, and savor life a bit more."*

"We haven't been able to see our children and grand-children as often as we'd like," said Mary. *"It's difficult for them to come to see us because of their jobs and the fact that their children are young. When Tim retires, we'll be able to go to them."*

"We're also thinking we'll have more time to do more here in town," said Tim. *"We've been talking about how we'd like to put something back into the community."*

Mary chimed in, *"We've had a wonderful life. Our children grew up in this town. They played baseball on the fields and went to the children's sports center. They learned to ride here. We'd like to help this community remain a good place for children."*

"Have you thought about a foundation?" asked Drew. *"You've got the money, and a foundation would make sense in your estate plan. Also, a foundation would let you give to charities and your church in the way you want. It would also let you change how the donations were made a year or two down the line."*

Tim and Mary looked at each other, intrigued by the idea, then looked back at Drew. *"We never even thought of it,"* said Tim. *"Can I ask a few questions?"*

"Absolutely," said Drew. *"But first, let me ask you an important question. Have you talked with your children about giving money to charities and the church?"*

Deciding on the Nature of Family Involvement

"Yes, we've talked with our children about it," said Mary. *"And they're all for it. They weren't surprised — they've seen us involved our entire lives, and expected we'd want to continue."*

"Of course, we want to be sure our children are taken care of," Tim added. *"And, we want to be sure that there's money for the grandchildren's education, but we've already covered that in the planning we've done together."*

"One of the great things about a foundation is that it can be a family affair," said Drew. *"You can include your children on the foundation's board and make the giving decisions together. I have set up several foundations for families that way. The families get together once a year, paid for by the foundation, to meet and make the decisions. A foundation is a great reason to have family reunions."*

"That sounds wonderful," said Mary. *"We've tried all sorts of things to carve out regular time together, but it has been difficult with all the things going on in our children's lives — they're so busy. A foundation may give us all that extra push."*

"I'd like to know more about private foundations before making a decision," cautioned Tim. *"How can we figure out if a foundation is for us?"*

"Let me look into it for you," said Drew. *"I'll do the numbers and put together some alternatives for you to look over."*

Doing a Financial Feasibility Study

Drew had most of Tim and Mary's financial data, but he updated it. The final financial profile looked something like this:

- Annual income: $500,000, consisting of salary and stock options

- $2.2 million in Tim's company pension plan

- $2 million in company stock and stock options he has zero basis in

- Their primary residence and a second home in Colorado

- Total assets of about $5 million

Drew looked over the numbers: Tim and Mary owned their own home and had enough built up in the pension fund to ensure a comfortable retirement. Their other assets met their goals for leaving something to the children. The big opportunity (and challenge from an estate- and tax-planning perspective) was the highly appreciated stock.

Drew decided that the clearest way to help Tim and Mary sort out their options was to present two alternative ways of giving to charity: one would be the foundation; the other would be selling the stock.

When Tim and Mary next met with Drew, he went over these alternatives in detail. This is the plan Drew presented for giving to charity by selling the stock:

Amount the Olsons would receive if they sold the stock now	$2,000,000
Their cost basis	0
Amount on which they would have to pay capital gains	$2,000,000
Amount they would have to pay in capital gains tax (20%)	$ 400,000
Amount left to invest	$1,600,000
Amount to give to charity each year if the investment made 8%	$ 128,000

Under this plan, Drew showed the Olsons how they could give $128,000 to charity every year. Drew added some additional notes about the income tax consequences of charitable giving both before and after retirement. He also added a note about the alternative of investing in tax-free municipals.

Then Drew presented the plan for giving to charity by creating a foundation:

Current value of the Olson's stock	$2,000,000
Their cost basis	0
Amount they could give to the foundation (in stock)	$2,000,000
Amount they would have to pay in capital gains tax (20%)	0
Amount left to invest	$2,000,000
Amount to charity each year if the investment made 8%	$160,000

Under this plan, Drew showed the Olsons how they could give more to charity. Drew told the Olsons that they had the option of giving the minimum to charity of 5% ($100,000) and adding the other $60,000 to the $2,000,000 in the foundation, so that the following year (and every year after that) the amount in the foundation would grow, assuming net returns were always more than 5%.

After talking with Tim and Mary for about an hour, Drew sketched out a chart and slipped it across the table.

"I think this is where we are," he said. *"Here are the pros and cons of each choice the way we've been talking about them. The way I see it, there's no right or wrong choice, it's whatever you're comfortable with."*

	Pros	Cons
Sale of Stock	Not committed to always using the income for charity	Big capital gains tax penalty
	Family could be involved informally in decisions	
Foundation	Bigger first year contribution possible	Permanent commitment
	Could build up principal	
	Family involvement formalized & subsidized	

"Take some time to think it over," suggested Drew. *"It's a big step. An exciting step, but a big one."*

Implementing the Foundation

A couple of days later, Tim telephoned Drew. *"Mary and I would like to do the foundation,"* he said. *"We like the idea that it could grow into the future. We like that it's a permanent sort of a thing, and that it could continue our family tradition with our children and grandchildren."* Tim paused, then said, *"What do we do now?"*

Creating the Legal Documents and Selecting an Administrator

"Let me get going on the documents," said Drew. *"Give me a couple of weeks, and I'll have something to show you."*

A month later, Tim and Mary met with Drew, made some changes and signed the final documents.

"Who are you going to select as your administrator?" Drew asked, putting the signed forms away in his briefcase.

Mary smiled. *"I'd like to do a lot of it personally,"* she said, *"With your office paralegal as a backup. I won't need any more help than that at the beginning, since we only want to give to the church and the youth program. We aren't asking for grant proposals or the like."*

Putting Together the Board

Tim and Mary had kept the children involved throughout the process, and all three children were interested in being on the board. They had their first complete family reunion in years at a resort hotel nearby, so Drew could come out and brief everybody on the idea of the foundation and what their responsibilities were as board members. The family met in the morning as the board, and socialized and played with grandchildren in the afternoons and evenings.

Selecting an Investment Advisor

Selecting an investment advisor for the foundation was simple. Tim turned to Adam, his personal financial planner and investment advisor. Tim had worked with Adam for years on his personal investment portfolio, and the two men had become close friends. Tim was even more sure of his choice when he found out that Adam was the investment advisor on several other foundations.

Transferring Assets

Given that Tim and Mary can only use a tax deduction of a maximum of 20% of their total income, donating the full amount to the foundation in one year would not allow them to take full advantage of their allowable deduction. With Drew's advice, they decided to contribute smaller amounts to the foundation every year, and leave any remainder to the foundation under their wills.

Beginning the Work of the Foundation

At their first meeting as a family foundation board, Tim and Mary took turns explaining their vision.

"This first year, we don't have a lot to give," Tim explained, *"But it's a start we're grateful we can make. Anyone have any ideas?"*

"Mom and Dad," said Mike, their oldest, *"We've talked about it, and want to help you do what you want to do. You've put a lot of care and effort into the youth group and the church — I guess we all expect you'll want to start from there."*

The other children chimed in and, after a little more discussion, the decision was made: they'd give half of the minimum donation to each. The difference between the minimum donation and the total income from investments (after the expenses of the reunion and the legal firm's paralegal) would be kept in the foundation's pool of funds so that the principal could grow.

Obeying the Rules of the Road

That night, after the reunion, when Mary and Tim were alone, Mary said, *"I'd love to give each of the children something. Didn't Drew say we could pay them from the foundation for being members of the board?"*

"Yes, he did, honey," said Tim, *"But I'd like to wait a little on that. Since we decided to put the money into the foundation more slowly, we have less money to give away in these first few years. I think it's enough that the foundation paid for a chance for all of us to get together. Remember, when Drew talked about the rules for a foundation, he cautioned us against making it look like some sort of dodge."*

Carrying on Your Legacy

Several months later, Mary came into Tim's study with a letter in her hands.

"Here's a wonderful note from the youth program," said Mary. *"They're renovating the club room with the donation we made and will rename it in our honor. They want us to come to the dedication ceremony."*

Tim grinned from ear to ear, then said in a bittersweet voice, *"I guess they'll paint over Evelyn's hand prints from the time we all pitched in and painted the clubroom...but I guess we'll always know where that spot is. Whatever day that ceremony is, we'll make it."*

Enjoying Your Legacy

A few years after the foundation was established, when it was time for another reunion, Mary said, *"Where shall we go this year? The first year we went to that place just outside of town. Last year we went to Colorado. What shall we do for an encore?"*

"I don't know," said Tim, *"But you could call the children and ask."* He paused, and said with a smile, *"It's a nice sort of problem to have, isn't it?"*

Case Study #2

The Thomas and Holly Ford Foundation: Funding a Foundation by Establishing a Charitable Remainder Trust

Holly Ford is a sixty-eight-year-old widow with two adult children and five grandchildren. Financially secure, Holly owns her home and comfortably lives off of her pension and social security benefits. Before her husband, Tom, died two years ago, Holly and Tom accumulated a large portfolio of publicly held stocks. The portfolio is worth 2 million dollars and has a cost basis of 500,000 dollars. In addition, her home and other assets total 250,000 dollars.

Deciding on the Legacy

In one of her meetings with Paul, her financial planner and long-time friend, Holly said, *"I'd like to do something for my church. While Tom was ill, and after he died, my church was an enormous support."*

"I remember," said Paul. *"More than once, now, you've expressed a desire to give to your church, and several other charitable organizations in the community as well. Perhaps now is the time for you to consider establishing some kind of a foundation."*

"What a good idea," said Holly. She paused, then looked a little worried and said, *"This won't substantially diminish my income, will it?"*

"Not in the least," said Paul. *"What it should do is increase your income and eliminate any unnecessary estate taxes."*

Deciding on the Nature of Family Involvement

"Sounds good," said Holly. *"I've been going round and round on ways to formally involve my family in this community. We've always been very active, but sometimes it's been rather haphazard. It would be nice to be a steady, dependable presence."*

"Next time you get together with your children," said Paul, *"discuss setting up a foundation and involving them on the*

board of directors. I also think you should consult with your other advisors to gather as many ideas as you can for how you want to approach setting up a foundation."

"Will do," said Holly. Looking very animated, she added, *"I haven't felt so gung ho in a long time. A foundation will give me a real focus, and I can work with my children. It can be a project we share."*

Doing a Foundation Feasibility Study

Holly gathered all her financial information and met with Paul. After going over her finances, he confirmed that she could indeed establish a foundation and that the most sensible way to do it was through her portfolio of publicly-held stocks. His suggestion was as follows:

Rather than earn only 2% income or $40,000 annually on the portfolio, Holly could earn income for life in the amount of 8% annually or $160,000 a year from a trust.

Implementing the Foundation

Holly met with Paul one morning over breakfast. *"I've settled on how I'd like to set up my foundation,"* she said. *"I'd like to establish a charitable remainder trust in combination with a private foundation."*

"Sounds sensible," said Paul. *"Let's go over the details."*

"The way I understand it is that my first step will be to contribute my publicly held stock into a charitable remainder trust," said Holly. *"The trust will pay me income for life in the amount of 8%, rather than the 2% I'm receiving now."*

"That's right," said Paul. *"And you'll receive an income tax deduction of approximately 20%, and will avoid the capital gains tax on $1,500,000, totaling $300,000."*

"And," Holly added with a smile, *"I won't have to be concerned with the estate tax on this amount, which would have totaled over $700,000."*

"You got it," said Paul. *"Your second step will be to set up*

a wealth replacement trust in the amount of 2 million dollars for your children. This trust will remain outside of your estate and will contain a life insurance policy."

"And I can set up this wealth replacement trust of 2 million dollars using income from the 2 million dollars I used to establish the charitable remainder trust," said Holly.

"Exactly," said Paul. *"Your third step will be to establish The Thomas and Holly Ford Foundation as the charitable remainder beneficiary of your trust. The Foundation will support in perpetuity the causes that you and your husband believed in."*

"The Thomas and Holly Ford Foundation," said Holly, *"I like the sound of that."* She wistfully smiled at Paul, and added, *"I only wish that Tom and I could have established the Foundation together."*

Creating the Legal Documents, Selecting an Administrator and an Investment Advisor

Paul referred Holly to an experienced lawyer whom he had known for a long time. The lawyer drew up the paperwork for the charitable remainder trust, the wealth replacement trust, and the private foundation.

Holly asked Paul if he would be the administrator for the trusts and the foundation, since she didn't feel comfortable shouldering the responsibility herself. Paul was happy to oblige, happy to help Holly create good works in the memory of his friend, Tom. Paul was also Holly's natural choice for the foundation's investment advisor, since he had been her financial planner for decades and had shown himself to be trustworthy and to possess good financial sense.

Putting Together the Board

Holly knew from her previous conversations with her children that they were keen to serve on the Foundation's board of directors. Since she and her children had already supported their church and various community organizations before, coordinating their effort, time and money, Holly knew that she and her children would work well together as a team.

Her oldest said, *"I've always liked working on projects with you, Mom."*

Her second child added, *"It'll be fun doing something constructive together on a regular basis."*

Beginning the Work of the Foundation

Holly and her children needed little discussion to settle on how they would distribute the foundation monies. They all agreed that they wanted to support the church counseling center that had provided Tom with such good emotional care near the end of his life. They furthermore decided that they would support various other church and community outreach programs to help people and families in need.

Enjoying the Legacy

"For me," said Holly, *"my involvement with the Foundation has been like an act of devotion — I just set out wanting to give, and I unexpectedly received so much more in return."*

Case Study #3

The Sadie and Sonny Lee Foundation: Using a Life Insurance Policy to Establish a Family Foundation

Sadie and Sonny Lee are both sixty years-of-age. Sonny has worked for the same company all of his adult working life and plans on retiring in the next few years. All four of their children are professionals and totally financially secure. With a relatively modest estate of just 2 million dollars, Sonny and Sadie would like to do something charitably significant in the future.

Deciding on the Legacy

Sonny and Sadie invited their children and grandchildren over one Saturday afternoon. Sonny grilled some steaks and chicken while the grandchildren played in the back yard. The family sat down to eat in the shade of a big maple tree.

When they were all through with their meal, Sonny said, *"Sadie and I wanted to discuss with you our idea of establishing a foundation. We wanted to talk about a way we could do that without compromising either our ability to look after ourselves..."*

"...Or our ability to help you out, if need be," said Sadie. *"Since you're all doing well on your own,"* said Sonny, *"and we have a significant pension plan from the company, it occurred to us that our life insurance policy of $500,000 is kind of superfluous."*

"Kind of very," said Debbie, their oldest daughter, with a laugh. *"We're all grown and can take care of ourselves now."*

"Exactly," said Sadie. *"We don't have the worry anymore of what we'd do to support you if something happened to either one or both of us..."*

"...So we were thinking about donating the life insurance policy to start a foundation," said Sonny.

The children all looked at each other.

"Seems like the logical thing to do," said Debbie.

"Yeah, why not?" said Mindy. *"Sounds great,"* said Danny, their youngest. *"What kind of focus would it have?"* said Robby, their oldest.

"Wow," said Sonny. *"I didn't think the idea would meet with so little resistance."*

"Why would we want to resist?" said Danny. *"You've never been big spenders, so when you want to do something, we know it must be well considered."*

"And we want to support you the way you supported us," said Robby, with a mischievous smile, *"even when, at first, you couldn't see the wisdom of our choices."*

Sonny laughed out loud and Sadie just shook her head, remembering at what loggerheads they and their children had sometimes been.

"What kind of crazy scheme do you have in mind?" said Robby, with a twinkle in his eye.

"We were thinking of scholarships," said Sonny. *"Without your education, none of you would be as successful as you are today."*

"We'd like to make it possible for more students to go into professional fields," said Sadie, *"so we thought that scholarships seemed like the natural choice."*

The children all looked at one another again, and nodded.

"All right," said Debbie. *"We're behind you one hundred percent."*

Deciding on the Nature of Family Involvement

"Great," said Sonny. *"Just remember you said that when we're all in a meeting haggling over whom to give the scholarships."*

"You mean you want us to be on the board with you?" said Mindy.

"That's right," said Sadie. *"We'd like each of you to be on the board of directors of the foundation."*

"Cool," said Danny. *"Can I smoke a big fat cigar?"*

"Get serious," said Debbie. *"The foundation will take some time and effort."*

"Anything's easy after a two-year-old, then twins," said Danny. He looked at his parents. *"When did you want to get going on the foundation?"*

"Just as soon as we talked with you," said Sonny, *"And got your go-ahead."* Sonny looked at the other children. *"Would you like to work with us on the board of directors?"*

The children all agreed and wanted to know what the next step would be.

"I think we need to get a foundation feasibility study done," said Sonny. *"We know we want to donate the life insurance policy, but there are several different ways we can do it."*

Doing a Foundation Feasibility Study

Sonny and Sadie met with Bert, their lawyer and financial advisor.

"How'd your meeting go with the kids?" said Bert.

"Couldn't have been better," said Sonny.

"I think this foundation will turn out to be even more fun than I expected," said Sadie.

Bert pulled out a summary of their finances. *"Let me give you a brief overview of how you could set up the foundation,"* he said. *"You will get a current income tax deduction about the amount of the cash value in your life insurance policy. You'll be able to deduct the full amount - maybe not all this year, but over time."*

"That's exactly right," said Bert. *"And what's nice about that is that you'll be able to make grants to charity immediately because of the cash build up in the policy. And when Sonny dies, the total death benefit will flow into the foundation so that larger grants can be made in the future."*

"That's what we want to happen," said Sonny, giving Sadie's hand a squeeze.

"If you'd like to continue making premium payments on the policy," said Bert. *"You can simply contribute the amount to the foundation and the foundation then makes the payments to the insurance company."*

"And will those unrestricted cash contributions be fully deductible up to the 30% limitation?" asked Sadie.

"They will," said Bert. *"You've been doing your homework."*

Sonny then said, *"For that matter, couldn't we also cash in the policy and invest the proceeds into other investments that could possibly grow faster than the build up in the policy?"*

"You could," said Bert. *"You'd have to decide whether the increased management would be worth the financial gain to you."*

"It's all a question of balance," said Sonny. *"There's also the option of exchanging the policy for a larger second-to-die policy on both of us. We could then have a 1 million dollar policy paid up instead of a 500,000 dollar policy. The caution here would be to make sure that the cash value would be sufficient to make the minimum distributions each year without blowing up the policy."*

"That's right," said Bert. He paused, and laughed. *"Why do you two even consult me? You seem to have all the angles covered. I should be the one paying you."*

"Go on," said Sadie. *"You've been a good teacher."*

Implementing the Foundation

Sadie and Sonny talked it over in Bert's office, and decided to simply donate the policy to the foundation and make the premium payments.

"We'll see how that goes," said Sonny. *"We can always make further adjustments later on, if need be."*

Creating the Legal Documents, Selecting an Administrator

"Give me a few weeks to do the documents," said Bert.

Sonny and Sadie signed the final documents in Bert's office about a month later. When they were there, Bert asked them who they would have as the foundation's administrator.

"Sadie and I will do it together," said Sonny. *"We still play bridge together, so doing the foundation together shouldn't be too hard."*

Putting Together the Board, Beginning the Work of the Foundation

The family formally met twice a year to do general foundation business and more often when making scholarship decisions. The children had a good sense of what to look for in scholarship applicants. Sonny and Sadie found that they all learned from each other when making the scholarship selections. The work of the foundation enriched their life as a family and gave them a new respect for each other's abilities.

Carrying on the Legacy

Sonny and Sadie's children have so enjoyed the work of the foundation that they are beginning to financially contribute to the foundation as well. Sonny and Sadie derive real satisfaction from knowing that they benefit other people's lives in a substantive way, and from knowing that their children know how good it feels to give.

Case Study #4

The Jennifer Green Foundation: Using Annual Contributions to Fund a Foundation

Jennifer Green, a successful cardiologist, is single with no children. At the hospital where she does her surgery, she has mentored quit a few young cardiologists. Her contributions to cardiology research have been many, and she has been a leading proponent of a holistic approach to remedying heart disease.

Deciding on the Legacy

During one of her rare vacations, Jennifer had time to reflect on the nature of her life and work. With her was Kaye, her college roommate now married with two teen-aged children. Jennifer and Kay sat on the balcony of their hotel room, sipping wine and staring out at Monterey Bay.

"I sometimes envy you, Kaye," said Jennifer. *"Sometimes I think, here I am saving lives, but I don't really have one of my own."*

Kaye shook her head with a little laugh, and said, *"Sometimes I feel that I don't have a life either — that all I do is make other people's lives work. I'll wager that my two teen-agers are a lot less grateful for my efforts than your patients are for yours."* Kaye paused, and corrected herself, *"It's not that I expect them to be grateful, it's just that I would have liked to pursue my own life more."*

Jennifer reached out and patted her friend's arm and said, *"From my perspective, you've made an authentic life for yourself, one that has heart."*

"Heart?" said Kaye, and she and Jennifer burst out laughing.

"I'm glad I didn't want to be a writer," said Jennifer. *"I would've disappointed myself big time."* Jennifer took another sip of wine, then said, *"Just hearing you talk about your kids, Kaye, makes me realize how much I want to leave something behind."*

"You're giving people another chance at life," said Kaye, *"that's an incredible thing to leave behind."*

Jennifer replied, *"What I mean is that I'd like to leave something behind that's larger than one person, me or anybody else. I'd like to leave something behind that's larger than the sum of its parts."* She paused, then said, *"I'd like to establish some sort of a foundation, something through which I could help support the hospital where I do my surgery."*

"Just for the hospital in general?" said Kaye.

Jennifer didn't answer right away. Then she said, *"More of an endowment of sorts for young researchers. It would be really satisfying to know that cardiologists who share my beliefs would have funding to build on the research I've done. It would be nice to provide real financial support to research into non-traditional approaches to curing heart disease."*

Kaye raised her glass to her friend. *"Sounds like a worthy endeavor,"* she said. *"Here's to your foundation."*

"Thanks, Kaye," said Jennifer. She and Kaye drank to the foundation.

"I admire you, Jennifer, and what you're doing," said Kaye. *"I'll help you in any way I can."*

"Ahh." said Jennifer. *"Now that you mention it, that gives me an idea."*

"What?" asked Kaye, somewhat suspiciously. *"I remember the time you had that great idea to go snow camping. We nearly froze to death."*

"We did have a lot of peace and solitude," said Jennifer.

"Solitude, I'll grant you," said Kaye, *"as for peace, I was worried the whole time!"*

"Oh well," said Jennifer, with a smile. *"nothing's perfect."*

"Tell me about it," said Kaye, and they laughed.

"No, seriously," said Jennifer, *"what if you were to be the administrator for the foundation?"*

"Me?" responded Kaye.

"Yes, you." said Jennifer. *"You're a Certified Public Accountant. You'd work with the foundation's board of directors. I know your attention to detail. You'd be great!"*

Kaye considered, then said, *"It's worth pursuing. It would be another way for us to be in contact."*

"And it would be a way for you to put more of your talents to work," said Jennifer.

"Sounds good," said Kaye. *"I'm all for that."*

Doing a Foundation Feasibility Study

When she returned from vacation, Jennifer met with her financial advisor to puzzle out how she could establish her own foundation. The most obvious solution was the one that she used: Her parents had left her a piece of real estate when they died. Valued at $250,000, the property could be used to fund the foundation, and would represent Jennifer's starting amount. She would be able to deduct the basis amount from her income up to a maximum of 20% each year until the full amount was used up, with a maximum of five additional tax years.

In addition, Jennifer decided to contribute $100,000 to the foundation each year that she was working, providing that her income remained consistent. In so doing, the cash gifts would be deductible.

Implementing the Foundation: Creating the Legal Documents, Putting Together the Board, Selecting an Investment Advisor

Through her financial advisor, Jennifer found a lawyer who drew up the paperwork. Jennifer selected a few of her proteges, all now successful cardiologists in their own right, to be on the board of her foundation. In selecting them, she knew that they would understand and implement her vision for the foundation. Kaye happily consented to be the foundation's administrator, and Jennifer's financial advisor agreed to be the investment advisor for the foundation.

Beginning the Work of the Foundation

At the first meeting of the board of directors, Jennifer and the other directors agreed that they wanted to fund cardiology research that was underfunded by national organizations. In particular, they wanted to fund more research into heart disease in women, and non-traditional approaches to cures. They agreed to accept grant proposals and to do the selection themselves. At the end of the meeting, they all felt deep satisfaction from knowing that, through the work of the foundation, they would contribute to one of the most fundamental and essential aspects of life.

Carrying on the Legacy

As specified in the Mission Statement for the foundation, Jennifer knew that the foundation would continue in the spirit of her research and beliefs. She felt a sense of contentment that she had never known before. Prior to establishing the foundation, she had always felt a sense of unfulfilled urgency in her research, as though she could never accomplish enough, quickly enough. Once the foundation was established, she felt a subtle, yet profound change occur within herself. She still felt driven to do her research and to strive for the best for her patients, yet the context in which these occurred had changed: now that she had established The Jennifer Green Foundation, she felt less pressure to "save the world" herself. Now that there was the foundation, she felt a profound sense of security in knowing that, no matter what, there would be others after her to carry on non-traditional types of research into the life of the heart.